DISCOVERING THE MEANING OF SCRIPTURE

Walking in the Way of Christ & the Apostles
Study Guide Series
Part 1, Book 4

An 8-Session Study

Peter Briggs

ISBN: 9781947642041

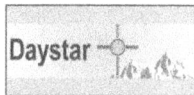

Published by:

Daystar Institute / NM, Inc.
P.O. Box 50567
Albuquerque, NM 87181-0567 USA
www.DaystarInstituteNM.us

Distributed in Africa by: Daystar Institute / Africa
Kampala, Uganda
www.DaystarInstituteAfrica.org

Table of Contents

Figures

WitW
Walking in the Way of
Christ & the Apostles

Foreword

Jesus Christ, in His three-year ministry with His twelve disciples, modeled the method for teaching disciples to walk in His way.

The Walking in the Way (WitW) Study Guide Series attempts to model Christ's method of teaching by utilizing a holistic approach designed to challenge students to apply biblical principles to their lives and ministries. Our aim is to equip disciples of Jesus to "walk in him, rooted and built up in him and established in the faith, just as you were taught, abounding in thanksgiving." Colossians 2:6,7. Thus, we emphasize wholehearted discipleship, practical Christian theology, and a biblical world view.

We have prayerfully designed the WitW study materials to equip you with the tools and concepts needed to achieve this goal. May the word of God dwell in our hearts richly through faith by studying it, reflecting upon it, and allowing it to penetrate the deepest recesses of our souls. By this means, we bring our hearts and minds into alignment with God's heart and mind.

How to Use this Study Guide

Although this Bible study may be done independently, we strongly recommend using it in a group setting. Study each session prayerfully and reflect deeply on the included passages of Scripture as part of your daily devotional time with God. Establish a journal in which you record your answers to questions, as well as your reflections and notes.

If you are participating in a group study, be prepared to interact with your leader and group members. This includes sharing insights and practical lessons God is teaching you personally.

Read the questions and associated Scripture passages aloud and stick to the Bible as your sole authority for answers given. At the end of each discussion session, take time to pray for group member needs; then hold one another accountable for putting the lessons learned into practice.

Upon completion of one book, move on to the next book in the series. In parallel, begin sharing the WitW teaching with family members, work associates, and others in your circle of influence.

Leaders may use their discretion as to how much material to cover in any given discussion session. We also encourage Bible study teachers and leaders to read the associated WitW Theological Handbook or Theological Reader in order to gain a better understanding of the material presented in this booklet. Our resources are listed in the back of this study guide and are available on Amazon.com.

Introduction to Book 4

In Book 3 of the WitW Part 1 Study Guide Series, we came to appreciate how critical biblical representations are for practicing the Christian life. Since the Bible is the sole source of biblical representations, the fact is evident that we must learn how to study the Bible for what it actually says, not for what we think it says. In other words, we want to discover the author's intended meaning. Only then can we correctly understand the theological, moral, and ethical principles that should govern our lives and ministries. Rightly understanding and interpreting biblical books and passages is critical to developing a biblical worldview.

Learning Objectives for Book 4

1. To learn how to apply the principles of biblical and exegetical theology in studying the Scriptures.

2. To understand that context holds the key to correctly determining a biblical author's intended meaning.

3. To appreciate the various literary styles or genres contained in the Bible.

Our desire is that every disciple of Jesus Christ be firmly rooted, built up, and established in his faith in accordance with Colossians 2:6-7. We have prayerfully designed the WitW study materials to equip you with the tools and concepts needed to achieve this goal. May the word of God dwell in our hearts richly through faith by studying it, reflecting upon it, and allowing it to penetrate into the deepest recesses of our souls. By this means, we bring our hearts and minds into alignment with God's heart and mind.

As you begin each lesson, pray that God would open your heart to the study of His word, that He would speak to you through His word, and that He would cause His Holy Spirit to use the word of God to break up the fallow ground of your hearts. This study is not about learning a lot of facts – it is about living out the truth of the Scripture in order to glorify God and impact others for the advancement of Christ's kingdom.

Notes & Reflections

Formulate a statement of your personal goals and objectives for this study of how to interpret Scripture. Also, make note of any additional insights or comments as you begin this study.

Session 1. Discovering the Meaning of Scripture

Have you ever wondered how to interpret a particular verse or passage of Scripture? This can sometimes be a daunting task.

The science and art of interpreting texts is called hermeneutics, and biblical hermeneutics is the branch of this science and art which governs how we should interpret the Bible. We all have a method of Bible study – our own personal hermeneutic if you will. But we all need a good one! Developing a correct hermeneutic so that we can rightly handle the word of truth is what this study guide is all about.

Over the course of the eight sessions that make up this study guide, we will learn how to study the Bible for what it says, not for what we think it says. In other words, we want to discover the author's intended meaning. Only then can we understand the theological, moral, and ethical principles that should govern our lives and ministries. This will help us in developing a biblical worldview.

Reading Scripture from God's Point of View

The Bible is a magnificent literary work. It is a collection of 66 books: 39 in the Old Testament and 27 in the New Testament, all authored by God, together with 40 human authors employing many different writing styles and literary genres. The Bible was written over a period of some 1,500 years, primarily in Hebrew, Aramaic, and Greek. Each book retains the imprint of its human author, and yet the Bible is a single, cohesive unit which represents the manifold wisdom of its Divine Author to receptive human minds.

Because the Bible is a supernatural book – God's love letter to mankind – it can only be understood through the illuminating ministry of the Holy Spirit. He enables us to read with understanding, and He causes Scripture to come alive in our minds and hearts. As we internalize God's message, the Holy Spirit uses the word of God to transform us into the image of Christ. The Bible becomes living, nourishing, sustaining, and powerful for us.

The Structure of the Bible: the Canon of Scripture

Have you ever wondered how the books of the Bible came to be included and ordered? The English word "canon" derives from the Greek kanon, which means a measuring rod or standard. In the case of the Old Testament documents, the Torah, or the five books of Moses, was the standard. As later documents surfaced, their correspondence with the teachings of Moses was assessed to determine whether or not they bore the marks of being divinely inspired. In the case of the New Testament documents, a direct connection with Jesus Christ was the principal standard. That is, was the author either one of the apostles, or was he closely connected to one of the apostles?

Generally speaking, the canon of Scripture consists of those documents that have been recognized by the people of God down through the centuries as bearing the marks of divine inspiration. The earliest complete listing of the books of the Bible in the order we have them today was presented in the Easter letter by Athanasius, bishop of Alexandria, in 367 AD.

Literary Background of the Bible

The Bible is divided into two major parts: the first part consists of 39 books and is commonly called the Old Testament; the second part consists of 27 books and is commonly called the New Testament.

The Old Testament tells God's story from creation to within a few hundred years of the birth of Christ. It was written over a period of approximately 1,000 years beginning in the 15th century BC and ending in the 5th century BC; therefore, its literary background involves a number of languages and scripts. There are two principal forms of the Old Testament on which our modern translations are based: first, the Masoretic Text of the Hebrew Scriptures, which was compiled ca. 1000 AD; and second, the Septuagint, which is the translation of the Hebrew Scriptures into Greek. In that preparation of the Septuagint was commenced in the late 4th century BC, it is based upon a Hebrew text that predates the Masoretic Text by well over 1,000 years.

Although the designation "Old Testament" might have been appropriate in the 17th century AD when the King James Bible was translated, language is fluid, and word meanings have changed over time. Unfortunately, the word "old" now carries the meaning of worn out, discarded, or no longer relevant. The word "testament" brings to mind the idea of proof that something is true, or the legally binding instructions having to do with the disposition of a person's assets after death. Accordingly, the Old Testament designation is misleading to the modern mind.

The New Testament picks up God's story from the birth of Christ to the end of time as we know it, culminating in a new heaven and earth. It was written in koine Greek, which is the form of the Greek language that was used in the spheres of civil discourse and commerce in the 1st century AD. In fact, koine Greek was the lingua franca of the Greco-Roman world of the 1st century AD.

The implication of the designation "New Testament" to the modern mind is that it replaces and supersedes the Old Testament. In fact, many Christians concentrate their study in the New Testament, and they are largely ignorant of the Old Testament.

As someone has well said,

> "The New is in the Old contained,
> the Old is in the New explained.
> The New is in the Old concealed,
> the Old is in the New revealed".

Therefore, in order to promote the understanding of the Bible as a cohesive literary work and as a single, continuous story, we choose to call the two major divisions of the Bible **the Hebrew Scriptures** and **the Christian Scriptures**. This is the terminology that will be employed throughout the WitW study.

Canonical Structure of the Hebrew Scriptures

According to the Christian tradition, the Hebrew Scriptures are grouped into five canonical sections as follows:

The Pentateuch, consisting of the five books of Moses – Genesis through Deuteronomy.

Historical Books, consisting of Joshua through Esther.

Poetic Books, consisting of Job through Song of Solomon. This section is sometimes referred to as the Wisdom Literature.

Major Prophets, consisting of Isaiah through Daniel.

Minor Prophets, consisting of Hosea through Malachi.

However, according to the Hebraic tradition, the Hebrew Scriptures are grouped into four canonical sections as follows:

The Torah, consisting of the five books of Moses – Genesis through Deuteronomy.

The Early Prophets, consisting of Joshua through 2nd Kings.

The Latter Prophets, consisting of Isaiah through Malachi, but not including Daniel.

The Writings, consisting of all the remaining books and ending with 2nd Chronicles.

Q 1.   What similarities and differences do you notice between these two groupings?

Q 2. One noteworthy difference is the Hebraic designation "Early Prophets" for the historical section of Joshua through 2nd Kings. What is the significance of this designation?

Q 3. Most of the books of the Hebrew Scriptures consist of narrative or stories. In fact, the Torah, Early Prophets, and much of the Writings are dominated by narrative. Why do you think God chose to communicate in narrative form?

For purposes of the WitW study, we choose to embrace the Hebraic tradition as set forth in the second list above. Accordingly, the Torah is the foundational section of the Hebrew Scriptures; in fact, it is the foundation of the entire Bible. Its stories provide answers to questions regarding origins, man's purpose, and his relationship with God. In other words, the Torah is the foundation for doctrine, and the other three sections of the Hebrew Scriptures serve as commentary on the Torah. For this reason, we refer to the Torah as **the fountainhead of wisdom.**

Canonical Structure of the Christian Scriptures

The canonical structure of the Christian Scriptures that we will employ throughout the WitW study consists of four sections as follows:

The Gospels and Acts, consisting of the four Gospels and the Book of Acts.

The Pauline Epistles, consisting of Romans through Philemon.

The General Epistles, consisting of Hebrews through Jude, but not including the three epistles of John.

The Johannine Literature, consisting of the three epistles of John and Revelation.

The first three Gospels – those of Matthew, Mark, and Luke – are commonly designated the **Synoptic Gospels** because their content is similar. John's Gospel, however, is decidedly different. In fact, some orderings of the Christian Scriptures lift John's Gospel out of the first section and include it in the last.

Q 4. What benefits derive from keeping John's Gospel in the first section?

Q 5. What is the logic of including the Book of Acts in the same canonical section as the four Gospels? What benefits derive from this grouping?

There is a noteworthy correspondence between the first canonical section of the Christian Scriptures and the first canonical section of the Hebrew Scriptures. First, both consist of five books. Second, even as the Torah records the story of the background of the nation of Israel, in like manner, the Four Gospels and the Book of Acts record the story of the background of the Christian faith.

Moreover, even as the other three canonical sections of the Hebrew Scriptures provide commentary on and develop the implications of the Torah, in like manner, the other three canonical sections of the Christian Scriptures provide commentary on and develop the implications of the Four Gospels and Acts – that is, the story of Christ's life, ministry, death, burial, and resurrection and the proclamation of the Christian gospel by the apostles.

True Narrative Supports Doctrine

A point that we need to emphasize is the nature of biblical narrative. In Book 2 of the WitW Part 1 Study Guide Series, we discussed the significance of the Bible as true narrative. Because the modern mind has become so accustomed to thinking of stories as fictional or even false, it is essential that we emphasize that the stories of the Bible are factual accounts of events that actually took place in history.

Figure 1 shows how the storyline that flows through both the Hebrew and Christian Scriptures supports doctrine – that is, the theological, moral, and ethical principles that should govern our lives and ministries. In other words, the Bible's story is primary, while the principles derived from the story are secondary. We are not saying that doctrine is unimportant, but rather that the authority of the doctrine depends upon and derives from the truthfulness and integrity of the story.

This approach is different from that of systematic theology, which tends to disconnect doctrine from the story, and thereby to disconnect it from people's lives, experience, and practice. It defines belief but not behavior. In fact, it can become a grid through which Scripture is read, thereby clouding the reader's understanding of the biblical author's intended meaning.

Narrative of the Hebrew Scriptures

Narrative of the Christian Scriptures

A
Σ

Doctrine from the Hebrew Scriptures

X

Doctrine from the Christian Scriptures

Ω

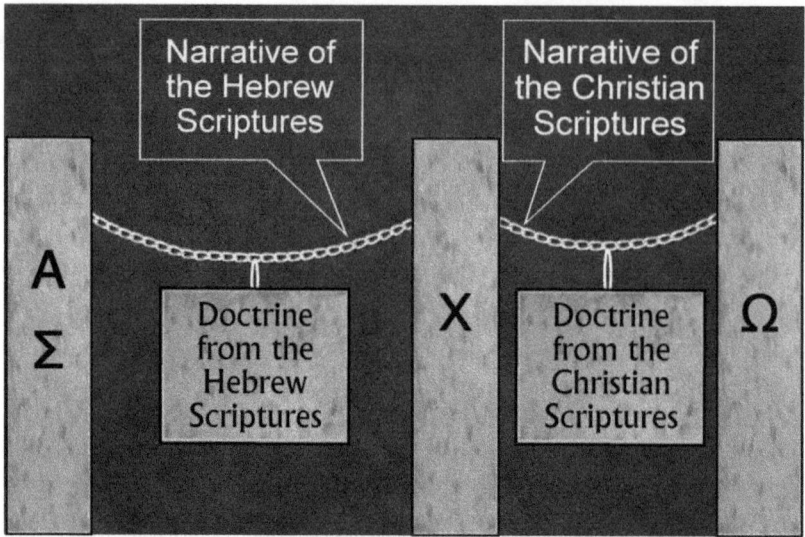

Figure 1. True Narrative Supports Doctrine

Another concept we discussed in Book 2 of the WitW Part 1 Study Guide Series was the definitions for the Greek letters in Figure 1. As a review, they are:

Alpha Event (Á) The creation of the cosmos by Yahweh Elohim, the Infinite Personal God who is really there.

Sigma Event (Σ) The invasion of evil, sin, and death into the terrestrial realm.

Chi Event (X) The Christ event – that is, the life, ministry, death, burial, and resurrection of Jesus Christ.

Omega Event (Ω) The end when Yahweh Elohim brings all things to their final consummation according to His will, and for His glory.

These four events impart meaning and significance to everything else in life, including all persons, events, circumstances, and things. The meaning and significance of our individual lives are entirely defined in relation to these four events.

Q 6. How has your life been impacted by the four events listed above?

One objective of this study guide is that we learn to regard the Hebrew Scriptures as Jesus did. And how did Jesus regard the Hebrew Scriptures? To answer this question, we turn to a statement by Christ in the 23rd chapter of Matthew, which records His stern rebuke of the Jewish leaders for the manner in which their predecessors persecuted the prophets. In this regard, He makes the following statement in the 35th verse:

> **Matthew 23:35**. So all the righteous blood shed on the earth will be charged to you, from the blood of righteous Abel to the blood of Zechariah, son of Berechiah, whom you murdered between the sanctuary and the altar.

To enable us to understand the historical significance of this statement, we need to remind ourselves that the last book in the Hebrew Canon is 2nd Chronicles, in which the stoning of Zechariah is recorded in 2 Chronicles 24:21. And of course the death of Abel at the hands of his brother, Cain, is recorded in the 4th chapter of Genesis, the first book in the Hebrew Canon.

Q 7. What is the implication of Jesus' statement in Matthew 23:35 regarding the historical factuality of the entire Hebrew Bible?

Notes & Reflections

Session 2. Appreciating the Biblical Text

If you were so inclined, you could take rigorous courses in hermeneutics to thoroughly learn the art and science of biblical interpretation. But we have good news for you! The Bible itself gives us the key governing principles for rightly handling, understanding, and interpreting Scripture. In this session we discuss each of the following seven biblically based principles for interpreting the language of Scripture:

The biblical text is God-breathed.

The biblical text is precious and delightful.

The biblical text is authoritative.

The author determines his intended meaning.

The biblical text is understandable.

The biblical text deserves our lifelong devotion.

We should approach the biblical text with humility and openness.

These seven principles are foundational to rightly handling and correctly teaching the word of truth in accordance with 2 Timothy 2:15. In the sections which follow, each of them are briefly unpacked.

The Biblical Text is God-Breathed

This principle is derived from the assertion by the Apostle Paul at the end of the 3rd chapter of 2nd Timothy:

> **2 Timothy 3:16-17.** All Scripture is inspired by God and is profitable for teaching, for rebuking, for correcting, for training in righteousness, so that the man of God may be complete, equipped for every good work.

15

The phrase "all Scripture" translates the Greek *pas graphe*, which literally means "every writing." The phrase "is inspired by God" translates a single Greek word, *theopneustos*, which literally means "God breathed."

Q 1.   Understanding that the Apostle Paul was referring to the Hebrew Scriptures in this passage, what is the significance of his declaration? What confidence does this impart to you about studying the Bible?

Q 2.   From the passage above, what is the scope of the Bible's teaching and its application?

Our next Scripture passage is found in the 1st chapter of 2nd Peter as follows:

> **2 Peter 1:20-21**. First of all, you should know this: No prophecy of Scripture comes from one's own interpretation, because no prophecy ever came by the will of man; instead, men spoke from God as they were moved by the Holy Spirit.

Q 3.   How does this passage complement 2 Timothy 3:16-17?

Q 4. If the apostles Paul and Peter were alive today, do you believe they would extend the scope of their assertions in 2 Timothy 3:16-17 and 2 Peter 1:20-21 to include the entire Bible? On what basis do you believe this?

The Biblical Text is Precious and Delightful

Support for this principle is presented by King David's beautiful testimony in the 19th Psalm as follows:

> **Psalm 19:7-11.** The Torah of Yahweh is perfect, reviving the   soul; the testimony of Yahweh is trustworthy, making wise the simple. The precepts of Yahweh are right, rejoicing the heart; the commandment of Yahweh is radiant, enlightening the eyes. The fear of Yahweh is pure, enduring forever; the judgments of Yahweh are true, and altogether righteous. More to be desired are they than gold, even much fine gold; Sweeter also than honey and drippings of the honeycomb. Moreover, by them is your servant warned; and in keeping them there is great reward.
> [Adapted from the ESV]

Q 5. Why did David consider the Torah of Yahweh to be so precious and delightful? Do you have reason to believe that Jesus also regarded the Torah of Yahweh as precious and delightful? Do you presently regard the Torah of Yahweh in this way? What steps do you need to take in order to appreciate the Torah of Yahweh as David did?

17

Some reasons you may have included in your answer to Question (5) are as follows:

The Torah was breathed out by God Himself.

The Torah expresses God's covenant relationship with His people.

The Torah codifies the origin of the cosmos and the ancient history of mankind.

The Torah marks out the way of wisdom that leads to life.

The Torah represents the lifestyle of a person who is wholly devoted to God – that is, one who loves God with his entire being.

In particular, the Torah represents the lifestyle of Jesus Christ, who is the only man whose life conformed to all its righteous requirements.

In fact, David's delight in the Torah of Yahweh reflects the attitude of Jesus Christ Himself.

Q 6. What would happen regarding our attitude toward the Torah of Yahweh as we come to have and to be governed by the mind of Christ in accordance with 1 Corinthians 2:16?

The Biblical Text is Authoritative

For support of this principle we turn to Christ's Sermon on the Mount recorded in the 5th through the 7th chapters of Matthew. In particular, Jesus states the following concerning the Torah:

Matthew 5:17-20. Don't assume that I came to destroy the Law or the Prophets. I did not come to destroy but to fulfill. For I assure you: Until heaven and earth pass away, not the smallest letter or one stroke of a letter will pass from the law until all things are accomplished. Therefore, whoever deprives of its authority one of the least of these commands and teaches people to do the same will be called least in the kingdom of heaven... For I tell you, unless your righteousness surpasses that of the scribes and Pharisees, you will never enter the kingdom of heaven. [Adapted from the ESV]

Q 7.   What is the main point of Jesus' teaching in this passage?

Q 8.   From this passage, what can you determine about Jesus' attitude toward the Torah?

Read Matthew 24:35, Matthew 28:18-20, and John 16:12-16.

Q 9.   What assertions from the lips of Jesus Christ concerning the authority of Scripture are contained in these verses, and why are they important?

Q 10. In all these verses Jesus confirms the authority of Scripture. If we come to have and to be governed by the mind of Christ in accordance with 1 Corinthians 2:16, what will be our attitude toward the contents of the Bible?

The Author Determines His Intended Meaning

Why do you suppose we emphasize the idea of understanding the author's intended meaning? Suppose you were to write a love letter to your beloved, sharing sweet intimacies as in the Song of Solomon. How would you respond if your beloved were to toss your letter aside as meaningless, or read into it things you never intended, changing your meaning completely? It is very important, then, that we make every effort to discover the author's intended meaning, because the author is sovereign over the meaning of the text, not the reader.

Evidence of the importance of this statement is found in the heresies that abound in Christendom. In large measure, these have arisen from people having imposed their own meanings on the biblical text, rather than carefully determining the meaning intended by the author of the text. The act of reading into the text something from our minds is expressed by the Greek word eisegesis. The opposite, exegesis, is allowing the text to speak for itself. Learning to perform exegesis correctly and to avoid eisegesis is the goal of this study guide.

In support of the principle that the author, not the reader, is sovereign over the meaning of the text, we turn again to the passage in 2 Peter.

> **2 Peter 1:19-21**. So we have the prophetic word strongly confirmed. You will do well to pay attention to it, as to a lamp shining in a dismal place, until the day dawns and the

morning star rises in our hearts. First of all, you should know this: No prophecy of Scripture comes from one's own interpretation, because no prophecy ever came by the will of man; instead, men spoke from God as they were moved by the Holy Spirit.

Q 11. What is the implication of this passage in regard to how we should read and interpret Scripture?

The Biblical Text is Understandable

In support of this principle, we summon the testimony of Moses in the 29th chapter of Deuteronomy as follows:

> **Deuteronomy 29:29**. The hidden things belong to Yahweh our Elohim, but the revealed things belong to us and our children forever, so that we may follow all the words of this law. [Adapted from the HCSB]

Q 12. Based upon Paul's statement in 2 Timothy 3:16-17 – a passage examined above – do we have warrant to extend the scope of "the revealed things" to include the entire Bible? What is the implication of Deuteronomy 29:29 regarding the role of fathers in leading their families in Bible study?

The fact that the revealed things belong to children should be a great encouragement to us to study the Scripture. The study of the Bible is not restricted to those who have a seminary education but is accessible to everyone who loves Yahweh and desires to walk in His way.

> **John 7:17**. If anyone wants to do God's will, he will know whether the teaching is from God or whether I am speaking on My own authority. [Adapted from the ESV]

Q 13. What is the implication of this verse, and how does it apply to the biblical text being understandable?

> **James 1:5**. Now if any of you lacks wisdom, he should ask God, who gives to all generously and without criticizing, and it will be given to him.

Q 14. What assurance do we find in this verse? How does James' assertion apply to the biblical text being understandable?

> **John 16:13**. When the Spirit of Truth comes, He will guide you into all the truth.

Q 15. How does this verse apply to our study of the biblical text? How does it apply to the biblical text being understandable?

We have no excuse for failing to understand the word of God. If we are having trouble understanding a passage, we should simply ask God to help us. God may not give us a dream or vision, but He promises to impart wisdom to our feeble minds so we can properly understand His word.

The Biblical Text Deserves Our Lifelong Devotion

> **Joshua 1:8**. This book of the Torah shall not depart from your mouth; you shall meditate on it and audibly recite it day and night, so that you may be careful to practice all that is written in it. For then you will make your way prosperous, and then you will have good success. [Adapted from the ESV]

The ESV translates the Hebrew word *hagah* as "meditate." However, the Hebrew implies much more than silent meditation. It not only involves thinking about a passage and mulling it over in our minds, but it also involves audible recitation, and therefore memorization. Thus, we have added the phrase "audibly recite it" to more fully communicate the meaning of *hagah*.

Q 16. Joshua 1:8 is part of Yahweh's personal instruction to Joshua at the time of his commissioning as the new leader of Israel in place of Moses. Based upon Paul's assertion in 2 Timothy 3:16-17 and Peter's assertion in 2 Peter 1:20-21, do we have warrant in applying the command of Joshua 1:8 to the entire Bible? What is the implication of this command in regard to the manner in which we should study Scripture?

Meditation is becoming more and more popular in our culture, but meditation on and audible recitation of the language of Scripture as mandated by Joshua 1:8 is rare among the people of God. The world's view of meditation is to focus on a single thing – breathing, for example – for a short period of time, usually 5-8 minutes.

Q 17. How does the world's definition of meditation compare with that mandated by Yahweh Himself in Joshua 1:8?

> **2 Peter 1:4**. ... By these He has given us very great and precious promises, so that through them you may share in the divine nature, escaping the corruption that is in the world because of evil desires.

Q 18. According to the Apostle Peter in this passage, what is the goal of all our spiritual exercises, and how should that encourage us to persevere in them throughout our entire lives?

Approaching the Biblical Text with Humility and Openness

Because the Bible is a supernatural book, it cannot be approached in the same manner as other books, whether it is being read devotionally or being studied. Carefully read each of the following passages and answer the associated questions.

> **1 Corinthians 2:14-16**. But the unbeliever does not welcome what comes from God's Spirit, because it is foolishness to him; he is not able to understand it since it is evaluated spiritually. 15 The spiritual person, however, can evaluate everything, yet he himself cannot be evaluated by anyone. 16 For who has known the Lord's mind, that he may instruct Him? But we have the mind of Christ.

The Greek word which is translated "the unbeliever" in the 14th verse is *psuchikos*, which means a person dominated by the things of the soul – that is, a soulish person. And the Greek word which is translated "the spiritual person" in the 15th verse is *pneumatikos*, which means a person who is dominated by the things of the spirit.

Q 19. How would you compare and contrast these two kinds of people? What is the key factor that is present in the spiritual person that enables him to understand the Bible?

Doctor / Patient Relationship

> **Hebrews 4:12-13**. For the word of God is living and effective and sharper than any double-edged sword, penetrating as far as the separation of soul and of spirit, joints and of marrow. It is able to judge ideas and thoughts of the heart. No creature is hidden from Him, but all things are naked and exposed to the eyes of Him to whom we must give account.

This passage brings to mind the doctor / patient relationship. In fact, we can visualize the Holy Spirit as the surgeon, the language of Scripture as the scalpel, and the mind of the reader as the patient on the operating table.

Q 20. How does the doctor / patient metaphor instruct us as to how we should orient our minds with respect to the biblical text?

> **Matthew 18:1-4**. At that time the disciples came to Jesus and said, "Who is greatest in the kingdom of heaven?" Then He called a child to Him and had him stand among them. "I assure you," He said, "unless you are converted and become like children, you will never enter the kingdom of heaven. Therefore, whoever humbles himself like this child – this one is the greatest in the kingdom of heaven."

From the manner in which this passage opens, the fact is evident that Jesus is pushing back against the prideful attitude of the disciples. He states that we cannot enter the kingdom of God unless we become like children.

Q 21. To what characteristic of children is Jesus pointing in this statement? What bearing does this passage have on the way in which we approach the Bible?

To conclude this part of our study, we set forth the following points in regard to reading and understanding Scripture:

> Our lifelong objective and quest is to have and to be governed by the mind of Christ.

> We should cultivate a heart attitude of delighting in the language of Scripture as King David did. One way to do this is through memorization.

> We should train our minds to be submissive and open to the authoritative text.

> As we open our Bibles to read or study, we should pray that the Holy Spirit will illuminate the text and enable us to understand what God wants to impart to us. And we can be

confident that He will do this very thing, if our hearts and minds are receptive and submissive.

We should train our minds to be inquisitive and committed to discovering the author's intended meaning as understood by his original audience.

At the conclusion of our reading or study on any given day, we should prayerfully ask what it is that God wants us to derive from our reading or study: a new step of obedience, a correction to an ungodly representation, or an offense that requires confession and repentance.

We should always recognize and take into account the immense linguistic and cultural chasm that exists between the human authors of the Bible and ourselves. At the conclusion of this study guide, we will offer suggestions as to available resources that can help to bridge this linguistic and cultural chasm.

Thus, we approach the Bible differently from any other book. Because the Bible is the true revelation of the wisdom of God, we are not at liberty to slice and dice, criticize, disregard, or in any other way rule over it. Instead, it rules over us.

Notes & Reflections

Use the space below to record additional insights and comments resulting from your studies thus far.

Session 3. Literary Genre and Context

The objective of reading the Bible is to understand the author's intended meaning. What is God saying through the human author? We are not to read the Bible according to what we think it should mean, but what the author is actually saying. In other words, we are not to read our own ideas into the biblical text, which is called *eisegesis*; instead, we must allow the language of Scripture speak for itself, which is called *exegesis*.

The two principal methods of Bible study to be practiced throughout the WitW study are book-by-book studies, which is called biblical theology, and passage-by-passage studies, which is called exegetical theology. A third method is topical or subject-oriented study, which might be useful in preparing a message or a Sunday School lesson. Whatever method of Bible study a person chooses, there are three rules which must be thoroughly understood and consistently practiced:

Context is key to determining the meaning of a passage.

Application always **follows** interpretation.

While a given passage may have **multiple applications**, it has only a **single meaning**.

In asserting the third rule, I am in nowise stating that the meaning of a given passage of Scripture is **simple**. While the author's intended meaning is singular, the layers and implications of that meaning may be manifold.

In the previous session, we learned that the Bible is unique because it is a supernatural book. In particular, the language of Scripture is God- breathed, and the illuminating ministry of the Holy Spirit is essential to human understanding. In this session, we begin to dig into the **literary structure** of the biblical text. In regard to structure, one of the ways in which the Bible is unique as a literary document is that it incorporates four principal **literary genres**: **narrative** or story, **poetry**, **didactic** or teaching literature, and **apocalyptic** or prophetic literature. In fact, a given biblical passage may incorporate multiple genres, such as narrative with embedded poetry, or teaching with embedded poetry.

> *Since the rules of interpretation are a function of literary genre, we must train our minds to switch gears, as it were, even within a given passage.*

The other aspect of literary structure that we will begin to unfold is context. In particular, any given word or phrase of the biblical text is enveloped by circles of context including the following: the immediate context, the context defined by the paragraph or section within a book, the context defined by the book, the context defined by the canonical section in which the book is located, and the context defined by the entire Bible.

Q 1.   Thumb through your Bible and make a list of specific passages which serve as examples of each of the four literary genres identified above. For example, the entire book of Ruth is narrative, and the beloved Psalm 23 is poetry. Attempt to identify passages that incorporate multiple genres. For example, Adam's speech concerning his wife is poetry, which is embedded into the narrative of the 2nd chapter of Genesis.

Something that you may have observed as you thumbed through your Bible is that most of the biblical text is narrative or story. Therefore, it is essential that we learn how to properly interpret narrative passages. In such passages, we can think of context as containing the keys to answering the news reporter's questions: who, what, where, when, why, and how? In particular, context enables us to recognize the plot of the story, the themes, the location, and any customs or historical events that enhance and enrich our understanding of the story. For example, the **levirate marriage custom** practiced throughout the ancient Near East is key to understanding the book of Ruth. According to this custom, if a man should die without children, the closest male relative of the deceased should take the woman as his wife; the first male offspring of this union would then be reckoned as the offspring of the deceased.

In the case of didactic or teaching literature, understanding word meanings is essential to our correctly interpreting the point that the author is intending to put forth. As is the case with English or any other modern language, any given word may have a range of meaning. And this is even more emphatically true of the ancient languages in which the Bible was written. The key to correctly interpreting a word or phrase in a teaching passage is to be found in the context of the passage, especially the paragraph or section in which the word or phrase is located.

> *In sum, context is key to meaning, but the way in which context governs meaning is a function of literary genre.*

Literary Genres of the Bible

Table 1 presents a summary of the literary genres to be found in the canonical sections of the Bible.

From Table 1, make note of the parallels in organization between the Hebrew and Christian Scriptures.

Q 2.   List the parallels that you observed.

Figure 2 Literary Genres of the Bible

Hebrew Scriptures		Christian Scriptures	
Torah	Mostly narrative with embedded poetry, covenants, and law codes	**Gospels & Acts**	Mostly narrative with embedded didactic
Early Prophets	Mostly narrative with embedded poetry	**Pauline Epistles**	Mostly didactic with embedded narrative and poetry
Latter Prophets	Narrative, poetry, and apocalyptic	**General Epistles**	Mostly didactic with embedded narrative and poetry
Writings	Poetry and narrative	**Johannine Literature**	Didactic and apocalyptic

Five Aspects of Context

There are actually five important aspects of context that guide the discovery of the author's intended meaning in any given biblical passage:

Theological. For a given biblical book or passage, what did the immediate or contemporary audience understand about God and His ways? That is, what theological light did the preceding books shed on the book under study?

Historical. At the time of the writing of a given biblical book, what was the geo-political situation?

Cultural. At the time of the writing of a given biblical book, what were the prevailing customs? How did people of that time live and do their work?

Canonical. Where is a given biblical book located in the canonical structure of the Bible? What is the significance of that canonical location?

32

Linguistic. For a given biblical book or passage, what literary genre or genres did the author employ to convey his meaning? In what language and script was it originally written? What figures of speech and word meanings require special attention to ensure the accurate translation of their meaning to a modern audience?

Q 3. Why is it important to consider each of these aspects of context when studying a given book or passage? What does each contribute to correctly interpreting the book or passage?

There are two ways of studying a passage of Scripture: from the inside out or from the outside in. Visualize a set of 6 concentric circles with the passage in question at the center, encircled by each layer of context as follows:

Ask contextual questions of the passage under study.

Consider the paragraph or section in which the passage is located.

Move to the chapter.

Move to the book.

Consider the canonical section in which the book is located.

Relate the passage in question to the overall storyline of the Bible.

Depending on the purpose of your study session, you may have occasion to work through the above list in reverse; that is, start with the Bible
storyline and progressively narrow your focus until you reach the desired passage.

Q 4.   Consider your favorite Bible story and analyze it for context. Explain your method of analysis and your conclusions regarding the story you chose.

Bible Study Methods

Some popular methods of Bible study are listed below:

Biblical theology. A book-by-book study of the Bible that seeks to understand the message intended by the author and understood by his contemporary audience.

Exegetical theology. A passage-by-passage study of the Bible which takes place within the context of a biblical book and which thereby augments and supports the biblical theology method above. It does so by narrowly focusing upon a particular passage within a book.

Inductive Bible study. This term designates the analytical process that lies at the heart of the biblical and exegetical theology methods. It consists of three phases: (1) Careful observation of the linguistic content of a book or passage; (2) Interpretation, which is the act of deriving the author's intended meaning from the linguistic data observed in phase 1; and (3) Application, which is the synthesis of governing principles for life and ministry that are presented by a book or passage.

Manuscript Bible study. This term designates an approach to Bible study that totally removes the chapter and verse structure, as well as chapter and paragraph headings, and focuses attention upon the inspired text without artificial embellishment. The manuscript method can be used to facilitate the observation phase of inductive Bible study.

Systematic theology. A topical study of the Bible, usually in accordance with a set of traditional systematic categories.

Deductive Bible study. This term designates the analytical process that lies at the heart of the systematic method whereby a doctrinal position is derived from a collection of biblical passages.

Word studies. A word study seeks to understand how a particular word encountered in a passage under study is used elsewhere in the Bible. A word study can support and augment any of the above methods of Bible study.

Regarding deductive Bible study, following is an illuminating quotation attributed to Harvey Bluedorn in a web-based article authored by Brandon Adams:

> Deductive or synthetic Bible study gathers propositions from Scripture and arranges them as premises in formal arguments which reason toward necessary doctrinal conclusions which may not otherwise have been stated in the Bible. In this way, it builds biblical doctrine. On the basic level, the gathering and arranging of Scripture to prove doctrines has already been done for the student. On the advanced level, the student researches these on his own.

Q 5. Consider each of the Bible study methods summarized above and describe your personal experience with each one. Based upon your own experience and what you have learned thus far in the WitW study, offer an assessment of the strengths and weaknesses of each of the methods.

Summary

Following is a list of rules for correct interpretation that summarize our studies in this session:

Pay careful attention to all aspects of context for a given biblical book or passage.

Train your mind to seek to understand the author's intended meaning as it would have been understood by his contemporary audience. Avoid reading into a given book or passage anything from your own mind, especially dogmatically held doctrinal positions.

Consider other related passages, especially those which are located near to the book or passage under study.

Consider whether or not the language used in the passage has changed in meaning over the course of time.

Put into practice whatever God reveals to you during each study session.

Notes & Reflections

Session 4. Interpreting Narrative Literature in the Bible

As we learned from our studies in Book 2, the Bible is a story – in fact, the true story of God and His interaction with His creation. Most of the Bible is narrative. Bible stories may be simple or complex, action-packed or detail-laden; all are designed to teach theological, moral, or ethical principles. It is from these stories that we derive the doctrines of Scripture. Because the stories are true, they are like a great chain supporting the weight of the doctrines. These are the teachings which we not only believe, but which we also practice and obey – normative principles that govern our entire lives and ministries.

The figure below is a repeat of Figure 1, which we discussed in Session 1; it illustrates the fact that the true narrative of Scripture supports the doctrinal content of Scripture.

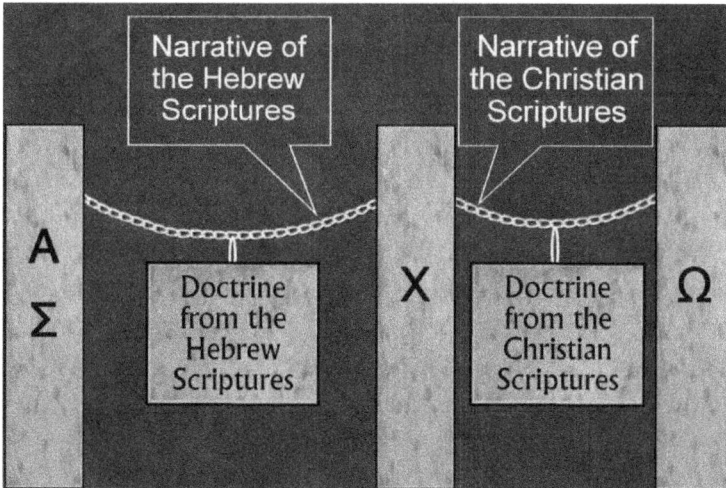

Q 1. What is your favorite Bible story and what doctrine can you derive from it? Are the doctrines you have identified normative – that is, are they applicable to all people, periods, and places, or are they bound to the particular cultural setting in which the story took place?

In general, a story is built around a plot line that consists of the following six elements:

Introduction or beginning

Problem

Crisis

Climax

Resolution

Conclusion

Q 2.   Choose a story with which you are familiar and share with your group each of the elements of that story.

Read 1 Samuel 17.

This passage records the David and Goliath episode, which we studied in Book 3 as an example of the life-critical importance of developing and maintaining a godly representational world.

Q 3.   Who are the main characters in this story? What do you learn about them through their words and actions?

Q 4.   What do you know about the time, place, and plot of this story?

Q 5.   Where is this story located in the Bible? Is it part of a bigger story? If so, explain.

Q 6.   Identify the beginning, problem, crisis, climax, resolution, and conclusion of the story.

Q 7.   What normative principles – that is, theological, moral, or ethical lessons that are applicable to all people, periods, and places – did you derive from the story?

Here are some things to notice in Bible stories:

Often characters tell the story without any moralizing on the story- teller's part.

Many biblical stories are streamlined – short and to the point.

Some biblical stories use techniques like repetition, dialogues, or significant speeches to emphasize important points.

Some biblical stories use key phrases to mark their beginning and ending.

Many biblical stories contain other literary genres, especially embedded poetry.

Read Genesis 2:4, 5:1, 10:1, and 11:10.

Q 8. What phrase is used in common in these verses, and for what purpose?

Q 9. Why is story telling so effective for people in general, and especially for those who live in an oral society? How can you take advantage of that fact in sharing the gospel?

Notes & Reflections

Session 5. Interpreting Poetic Literature in the Bible

Poetry is a beautiful means of expression. Ancient rabbis believed that if something was
worth saying, it was worth saying beautifully. That is certainly true of the poetry we find in the Bible.

Poetry is also memorable. In an oral society, learning comes through hearing and repetitive recitation. Because poetry can easily be set to music, the ancients learned the Bible by singing it – especially the Torah and the Psalms.

Poetry is readily recognizable in many modern English Bibles because each verse is indented. In your own Bible, compare the formatting of the Book of Psalms with that of the Book of Joshua.

Q 1.   Identify three Psalms that especially appeal to your heart and emotions. What is it about these three Psalms that causes you to respond in this way?

Q 2.   How can you recognize poetry in your Bible? List some books that are entirely poetry.

Hebrew poetry is different from English poetry. Hebrew poets were more interested in the rhythm and rhyme of ideas and thoughts rather than the rhythm and rhyme of sounds. This is fortunate for us since most of us cannot read biblical Hebrew, so we would not hear the rhythm and rhyme of sounds. But, even after translation into English, we can observe, understand, and appreciate thoughts and ideas, and how they are put together to create a thought rhythm or rhyme.

A significant difference between Hebrew and Western thought is in the area of logic. Western arguments generally build up to a conclusion, whereas Hebrew thought may surround their conclusion with their argument. Watch for examples of this type of expression.

Because Hebrew poetry is somewhat complex, we will take a closer look at its construction. Being able to recognize the structure of a given passage will help you to understand more quickly what the author intends to say.

Line. A single line of Hebrew poetry expresses a theological idea or concept.

Strophe. A strophe or strophic unit consists of one or more lines that are often presented as a single verse in our English Bibles. The multiple lines relate to one another in accordance with a concept called **parallelism**.

Parallelism. Parallelism describes the relationship between the multiple lines in a strophe. In the following paragraphs, we will touch upon several forms of parallelism. Parallelism not only imparts esthetic beauty, but it also enriches and adds emphasis to the communication of important theological concepts.

Complementary thoughts. The technical term for this kind of parallelism is synonymic parallelism. Even as a synonym is a word that means the same thing as another word, in synonymic parallelism the second line means the same thing as the first line. In other words, the first line in a strophe expresses a theological concept, and then the second line repeats that concept in somewhat different words. Consider the following example from the 119th Psalm:

Psalm 119:105. Your word is a lamp for my feet and a light on my path.

42

Q 3. The word "lamp" in the first line corresponds to "light" in the second line; and "my feet" in the first line corresponds to "my path" in the second. Recognizing that the Psalmist had in mind a small oil lamp, what theological concept was he communicating by means of this strophe? How do the two lines in the strophe work together to clarify and enrich our understanding of this concept?

Consider another example from the 102nd Psalm:

> **Psalm 102:1.** Yahweh, hear my prayer;
> let my cry for help come before You.
> [Adapted from the HCSB]

Q 4. What concept is expressed in the two lines of this strophe, and how do the two lines work together to enrich your understanding of that concept?

Q 5. Identify three other examples of complementary parallelism from the Book of Psalms and the Book of Proverbs and analyze each example in a manner similar to the analyses called for in questions (3) and (4) above.

- **Clarified thought.** The technical term for this kind of parallelism is **synthetic parallelism**. The distinction between synonymic and synthetic parallelism is not sharp. In the case of synthetic parallelism, the theological concept expressed in the first line of a strophe is not merely repeated in the second line with different words; instead, the second line significantly expands and adds richness to the expression of that concept.

Consider the following example:

> **Psalm 42:1-2.** As the deer pants for flowing streams,
> so pants my soul for you, O Yahweh.
> My soul thirsts for Yahweh, for the living Elohim.
> When shall I come and appear before Yahweh?
> [Adapted from the HCSB]

Q 6. This passage consists of three strophic units: the first two consist of two lines each, and the third consists of a single line. What concept is the psalmist is expressing in this passage?

Q 7. How do the multiple lines work together to expand and enrich your understanding of that concept?

Contrasting thought. The technical term for this kind of parallelism is **antithetic parallelism**. Even as a thesis and antithesis present opposing ideas, in like manner the second line of the strophe expresses a theological concept which is opposite to that expressed by the first line in this kind of parallelism. Consider the following example from the 1st Psalm:

Psalm 1:6. For Yahweh watches over the way of the righteous, but the way of the wicked leads to ruin.
[Adapted from the HCSB]

Q 8. What is the overall theological concept being communicated by the Psalmist in this strophic unit? How do the contrasting lines in the strophe work together to forcefully communicate this overall concept?

Q 9. List three more examples of antithetic parallelism from the Book of Psalms and the Book of Proverbs and analyze each according to the pattern of question (8) above.

Chiastic parallelism. The word chiastic comes from the Greek capital letter chi, which is **X**. The structure of a chiastic strophe can be diagramed as follows:

Line 1: Idea A
      Line 2: Idea B
            Line 3: Hinge idea C, central and most important
      Line 4: Idea B' = variation on B
Line 5: Idea A' = variation on A

Note that the structure of the strophe is designed to focus the reader's attention upon the hinge idea, C. Think of it like folding a piece of tracing paper at this central idea, so the other ideas would then appear on top of one another. Consider the following strophe from the 55th chapter of Isaiah:

45

Isaiah 55:8-9

"For My thoughts are not your thoughts,
and your ways are not My ways." This is Yahweh's
declaration.
"For as heaven is higher than earth,
so My ways are higher than your ways,
and My thoughts than your thoughts."
[Adapted from the HCSB]

Q 10. Identify each line of this strophic unit with the appropriate line label – that is, A, B, C, etc. Then reformat the entire strophe so that the indentation places in evidence the chiastic structure.

Q 11. In your own words, state the theological concept being communicated by...

Line A and line A'.
Line B and line B'.
Line C.

What is the subtle turn of phrasing that the Psalmist uses in lines A and B, and what impact does this have upon you, the reader?

Q 12. What is the overall theological concept being communicated by this strophe, and how do the lines in the chiastic structure work together to powerfully communicate this concept?

The fact that the main idea, or climax, in a chiastic structure is not at the end of the writer's progression of thought is important to recognize and remember. Understanding chiastic structures sensitizes us to recognize them and helps us to know where to look to find the author's key point.

Read Daniel 2-7.
Chiastic structure is not limited to poetry. Moreover, large chunks of Scripture can be arranged as a chiasm, as exemplified by chapters 2 – 7 of Daniel's prophesy.

Q 13. Identify the chiastic elements in this narrative:

    A
        B
                C
                C
        B
    A

Notice how the author moves from the A idea (visions) to the B idea (persecution of the messenger) to the C idea (pride and the associated downfall).

Q 14. What is the impact on you, the reader, as you consider the narrative of the 4th chapter of Daniel alongside of that of the 5th chapter within the framework of the chiastic structure diagramed above?

The formulation of chiastic structures, whether in poetry or narrative, require much more thought and skill on the part of the author. And as we learn to recognize and understand such structures, our appreciation for the literary beauty and richness of the Bible is greatly enhanced.

Q 15. Analyze the way in which chiastic construction is different from the Western approach to logic?

The use of poetry is not limited to the Hebrew Scriptures. Here is a list of some examples from the Christian Scriptures:

The Beatitudes. Matthew 5:3-10.

Christological hymns (that is, hymns about Christ). 1 Corinthians 15:3-8, Philippians 2:5-11, Colossians 1:15-20, Titus 3:4-7, 1 John 1:1-4; and 1 John 2:12-14.

Hymns of adoration. Revelation 4:8b, 4:11, 5:9-10; 12:12, and 13:10.

Q 16. How does understanding Hebrew poetry help you in reading the poetry of the Christian Scriptures?

Q 17. What questions might you ask to determine the context of a Hebrew poem?

For example, you might attempt to identify the author, the historical context of the passage – especially in the case of the Davidic Psalms – where the passage is located in revelation history, what kind of poetry it is (praise, lament, etc.), and other similar passages. Many of the Davidic Psalms were inspired by an identifiable episode in David's life experience. For example, Psalm 3 relates to the episode when David was fleeing from his son Absalom, which is recorded in 2 Samuel 15-18.

We have only scratched the surface of Hebrew poetry. Other types of parallelism which we haven't discussed include repetitive-additive, climactic, emblematic, mixed, and acrostic.

Q 18. How does understanding the structure of Hebrew poetry enable you to appreciate and value it more?

Because poetry is so much easier to remember than prose, we challenge you to memorize some of the Psalms, beginning with those that are most meaningful to you.

49

Notes & Reflections

Session 6. Interpreting Didactic Literature in the Bible

The technical term didactic derives from the Greek word *didache*, which means "teaching" or "instruction." In fact, the early church fathers produced a document called *The Didache* which provided new believers with the essentials they needed to know about living out their faith.

Q 1.   Where would you turn in the Bible to find examples of teaching literature?

Teaching literature dominates the Christian Scriptures from the Book of Romans through Jude. This is where we generally go to learn doctrine, because these books present theological, moral, and ethical principles clearly and directly instead of through poetry or stories. Teaching literature is more like a textbook than any other biblical genre.

Figure 1, together with the associated discussion, makes the point that the true narrative of Scripture is primary, and it supports the doctrinal content of Scripture. Accordingly, the teaching sections of Scripture serve as a commentary on the narrative sections. The epistles, therefore, take the form of a commentary on the Gospels and the Book of Acts. They expand, explain, and apply the teachings of Jesus and His apostles to the practice of life and ministry by the individual disciple and by the church as a corporate body.

The authors of the teaching books express their teaching in units of thought, or paragraphs. Most modern translations present the material in paragraph form, making it easier for the reader to grasp units of thoughts. However, a word of caution is in order. Verse, paragraph, and chapter breaks were not in the original manuscripts, but are the product of human scholarship. In some instances, chapter breaks are misplaced, and paragraph headings sometimes fall short of accurately representing the theological content of the paragraph. Therefore, we must always look to the text itself as the primary determinant of the author's intended message.

Context Determines Meaning

Because we are so intent on studying units of thoughts, or paragraphs, we should always read words, phrases, and sentences as elements of a paragraph rather than lifting them out of their paragraph context. In addition, the literary context of a given paragraph is defined by the paragraphs immediately preceding and following it. In particular, illumination of challenging word meanings can often be discovered by checking the manner in which a given word is employed in nearby contexts.

Always remember that context determines meaning.

Let's consider Philippians 4:13 as an example of the importance of context as the determinant of meaning.

> **Philippians 4:13**. I am able to do all things through Him who strengthens me.

Q 2. What is the common application of this verse?

Q 3. What is Paul's main point in the paragraph where this verse is located – that is, Philippians 4:10-13.

Q 4. What sentence of this paragraph best expresses Paul's main point?

Regrettably, the common English translation of Philippians 4:13 actually obscures Paul's intended meaning. Following is the rendering of this verse in *The New Testament: An Expanded Translation* by Kenneth Wuest, which comes much closer to expressing Paul's intended meaning:

> I am strong for all things in the One who constantly infuses strength in me.

Q 5. Based on what you have learned, what is Paul's intended meaning in the 13th verse, and how does it compare with your answer to question (2) above?

Q 6. Philippians 4:13 is used by Christians the world over to convey the idea that God can empower us to do anything at all through Christ. What conclusion did you draw from your study of this passage?

Much of Paul's letter to the Philippians has the tone of a letter from a missionary to one of his supporting churches, and this is especially true of the 4th chapter. In the paragraph in question, Paul is expressing his deep gratitude for the financial support he had recently received from the Philippian disciples. The 12th verse expresses his main idea – that he has learned to be content in all circumstances regardless of finances. How? By means of the strength that Christ constantly infuses within him. What then is Paul's point? God gives us the strength to be content in all circumstances. Would you not agree that is far different from common interpretation of the 13th verse? How does this teaching align with that of Isaiah 40:28-31?

Here is another example of how context determines meaning. Take the Greek word *sarx*, which is usually translated "flesh." With respect to mankind, there are three principal meanings of *sarx* that apply to the Christian Scriptures: (1) the soft substance of the body that covers the bones and is permeated by blood; (2) the human body; and (3) the unregenerated nature of man that is inclined toward evil.

The 5th chapter of Galatians is one of the principal passages that sets forth the teaching of the Apostle Paul on the conflict between flesh and Spirit. In particular, consider the 16th verse as follows:

> **Galatians 5:16**. I say then, walk by the Spirit and you will not carry out the desire of the flesh (= sarx).

Q 7. Which of the possible meanings of the word sarx best fits the context of this verse?

Now let's consider another passage in the Galatians letter.

> **Galatians 2:20**. It is no longer I who live, but Christ who lives in me. And the life I now live in the flesh (= sarx) I live by the faith of the Son of God, who loved me and gave himself for me. [Adapted from the ESV]

Q 8. Which meaning of flesh works best in this verse?

We submit that the third meaning above – the unregenerated nature of man that is inclined toward evil – is the meaning intended by Paul in Galatians 5:16, and the second meaning – the human body – is the intended meaning in Galatians 2:20. Thus, context determines meaning, and we must be careful not to assume a given biblical word always carries the same meaning.

Watch Those Verbs!

Verbs are the action words in sentences. Correctly identifying them in a sentence or passage is a very helpful way of determining meaning. Following is an outline of the method called verbal purview.

Determine the main verb – the word that represents the action.

Watch out for verbs that are preceded by the little word "to." They are called **infinitives** and are never the main verb.

Watch out for verbs that end in "ing." They are called **gerunds,** and they are never the main verb.

Watch out for verbs that introduce phrases which modify the main verb.

Let's consider Colossians 2:6-7 as an example application of the verbal purview method:

Colossians 2:6-7. Therefore, as you have received Christ Jesus the Lord, walk in Him, rooted and built up in Him and established in the faith, just as you were taught, overflowing with gratitude.

Q 9.   List all the verbs in this passage.

Q 10. Which one is the main verb?

Q 11. Based on your analysis of the verbs, what does this passage mean?

Perhaps you recognized this as our keynote Scripture passage for the entire WitW study. If you determined that **walk** is the main action verb in this passage, you are correct. The verbs "rooted," "built up," and "established" modify the verb "walk;" in other words, they enrich and expand our understanding of how we are to walk. "Received" is a past participle indicating action completed, and the phrase that includes it qualifies the main verb, "walk;" this is also true of "taught" and the phrase that includes it. The gerund "overflowing" and the phrase that includes it describes the outcome of the main verb walk.

Q 12. By what means did we receive Christ Jesus the Lord? By what means are we to walk in Him?

Grammatical Structure

Understanding the grammatical structure of a given passage gives greater insight into the meaning the author is intending to convey. Here we are looking at the words the author chose, their meaning as determined by context, and their function within a sentence. You will want to identify the subject, predicate, modifying phrases, etc. Because some aspects of grammatical structure are not susceptible to literal translation into English, including noun cases and verb tenses, it is important to select a good translation for your study Bible. Here is where you have opportunity to actually practice the skills you learned in English classes, such as in diagraming sentences. You will be surprised at what insights will arise from the sacred text as you closely examine and carefully analyze it.

Q 13. Select a verse with which you are familiar and experiment with diagraming it.

Q 14. Prior to the exercise of diagraming the verse, what was your understanding of its meaning? Did anything change as a result of the diagraming exercise? If so, what?

Interpreting Scripture with Scripture

When attempting to interpret a particular word, phrase, or term, it is important to use Scripture to interpret Scripture. Think of the ripple effect of a pebble tossed into a pond.

Examine the immediate context – that is, the paragraph – where the word, phrase, or term occurs for clues as to its meaning.

The second circle of context would be the paragraphs immediately preceding and following the paragraph in question.

The third circle of context would be the book where the paragraph in question is located.

The fourth circle of context would be the other biblical books authored by the same person as the book under study.

The fifth circle of context would be the canonical section where the book is located.

Finally, the sixth circle of context would be the whole Bible.

Let's consider 1 Corinthians 13:9-10 to exemplify using Scripture to interpret Scripture. In the HCSB, this passage is rendered as follows:

> For we know in part, and we prophesy in part. But when the perfect comes, the partial will come to an end.

It appears that the HCSB translation team was motivated to maintain a close correspondence with the King James rendering of this passage, which is as follows:

> For we know in part, and we prophesy in part. But when that which is perfect is come, then that which is in part shall be done away.

Now the 13th chapter of 1 Corinthians is part of a section of the epistle in which the Apostle Paul is addressing the exercise of spiritual gifts within the local assembly of God's people. This section of the epistle extends from the beginning of the 12th chapter through the 14th chapter. And so we must interpret the 13th chapter within this larger context.

In 1 Corinthians 13:9, the phrase "in part" translates the Greek phrase *ek meros*. Can we find an occurrence of *ek meros* somewhere else in the section under study? Yes we can, in 1 Corinthians 12:27, where it is translated "individually" as follows:

> Now you are the body of Christ and individually (= ek meros) members of it. [ESV]

In 1 Corinthians 13:10, "perfect" translates the Greek *teleios*, which is employed in 1 Corinthians 14:20 to mean "mature."

> Brothers, do not be children in your thinking. Be infants in evil, but in your thinking be mature (= teleios). [ESV]

Q 15. What contribution does this illumination from nearby contexts impart to your understanding of 1 Corinthians 13:9-10, and, in fact to the entire 13th chapter?

With this illumination of 1 Corinthians 13:9-10 from the two nearby contexts, the whole significance of this great chapter on self-sacrificing love comes into focus. Apart from that illumination, the 13th chapter comes across as a beautiful but unrelated parenthesis that interrupts the discussion of the exercise of spiritual gifts begun in the 12th chapter and concluded in the 14th. However, with that illumination, the important contribution of the 13th chapter to the discussion becomes clear.

The exercise of spiritual gifts – especially of tongues or languages – individually, and without concern for the edification of the entire body, is a sign of **immaturity**, which, in fact, was rampant within the Corinthian church. However, with maturity, **self-sacrificing love** comes to govern the exercise of spiritual gifts for the edification of the entire body and not as an expression of individual pride. In fact, the presence or absence of self-sacrificing love is the conclusive test of the genuineness of spiritual gifts. The faith of Jesus Christ and the ministry of the Holy Spirit operating in a disciple invariably causes his spiritual gifts to be exercised out of love for the body and with a view toward the body's edification, and never individually as an expression of human pride.

The Ordering of the Epistles

The epistles of the Christian Scriptures represent the greatest concentration of teaching in the entire Bible. Have you ever wondered about the chronological order of the epistles? One might expect them to be in chronological order, but they are actually ordered by length.

Consider first the epistles written by the Apostle Paul. According to their ordering in our Bibles, there are two major groupings. The first group is addressed to church communities, with the longest letter first – the epistle to the Romans – and the shortest – 2 Thessalonians – last. The second group is addressed to individuals, with the longest – 1 Timothy – first, and the shortest – Philemon – last.

Now consider the general epistles: Hebrews, James, 1 Peter, and 2 Peter. They are also ordered according to length. The three epistles by John are grouped together, and they are ordered by length. The last epistle is that of Jude, and it follows 3 John.

Returning to the Pauline Epistles – those written by the Apostle Paul – the ordering by length actually obscures both the chronological ordering and the trajectory of Paul's teaching. As illustrated in Figure 2, there are actually three chronological groupings of Paul's epistles as follows:

The early group, consisting of six epistles.

The middle group, consisting of three epistles.

The late group, consisting of three epistles.

Late Epistles
Ordering of
Churches

Middle Epistles
Establishment of
Churches

Early Epistles
Establishment of
Believers

Start of 1st
Missionary
Journey

1st
Imprisonment

2nd
Imprisonment
& Execution

Timeline of Paul's Ministry

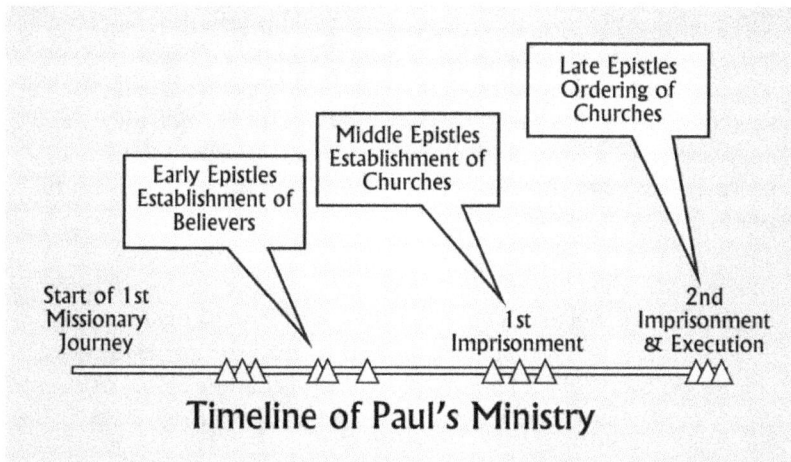

Figure 3. Trajectory of the Pauline Epistles

The short, personal letter to Philemon is a special case, and is associated with the letter to the church at Colossae, of which Philemon was a prominent leader.

As a result of careful study of twelve epistles of the Apostle Paul represented in Figure 2, we come to recognize the following:

> The six early epistles, consisting of Galatians, 1 & 2 Thessalonians, 1 & 2 Corinthians, and Romans, in that chronological order, are focused primarily on establishing **individual disciples** in a thorough understanding of the Christian gospel and its application to life and ministry.

> The middle epistles, consisting of Ephesians, Philippians, and Colossians / Philemon, are focused primarily upon establishing **church communities** in a thorough understanding of the Christian gospel and its application to life and ministry.

> The late epistles, consisting of 1 Timothy, Titus, and 2 Timothy, in that order, are focused primarily upon **ordering church communities** with qualified leaders.

The middle epistles are also called the **prison epistles**, since they were written during Paul's first imprisonment, the beginning of which is recorded by Luke in the concluding chapters of Acts. The late epistles are also called the **pastoral epistles**, since they were addressed to Timothy and Titus in their role as Paul's apostolic representatives to the church at Ephesus and the churches on the island of Crete, respectively.

In the last study guide in the WitW Study Guide Series – Part 3, Book 17 – we will examine the contents of Paul's epistles with greater care. Also, you are encouraged to read the corresponding chapter in the WitW Theological Reader – chapter 17 of TR3 – to check out the rationale for the chronological ordering of Paul's epistles.

Notes & Reflections

Session 7. Interpreting Apocalyptic Literature in the Bible

Apocalyptic is a technical term that derives from the Greek word *apokalypsis*, which means an unveiling, disclosure or revelation. In fact, this very word is employed by the Apostle John in Revelation 1:1, where it is translated "revelation." Apocalyptic literature is highly figurative and symbolic, using word pictures to convey meaning. It is also generally prophetical in nature.

The gift of prophecy enables a person to speak on behalf of God to the people of God. There are two types of prophecy: forth-telling or declarative, and foretelling or predictive.

> **Forth-telling,** or declarative prophecy, consists of warnings to the people of God concerning the spiritual, moral, and ethical implications of their present behaviors. Much of Isaiah and Jeremiah is declarative prophecy which focused on the judgment of God that would be the inevitable result of persistent immorality, especially idolatry.

> **Foretelling**, or predictive prophecy, deals with events that are future in relation to the time of writing. Prominent examples are the prophecies of Ezekiel, Daniel, Zechariah, and the Apostle John in the Book of the Revelation. Predictive prophecy is often apocalyptic in that it is filled with symbols, vivid imagery, and compelling word pictures.

In general, prophets viewed time in terms of two segments: the **present age** and the **age to come**. An example of this segmentation of time is seen in the glorified Christ's command to the Apostle John recorded in Revelation 1:19 as follows:

> **Revelation 1:19**. Write what you have seen, what is, and what will take place after this.

Figure 3 illustrates another aspect of prophecy: partial fulfillment in the near-term, and complete fulfillment in the far-term – that is, in the eschaton or end times. From the prophet's perspective, these are like two mountain ranges viewed from a distance through a pair of binoculars or telephoto camera lens. Although there may be a significant distance separating the two ranges, they appear as a single range when viewed in this way. In like manner, there are many instances in Scripture where the near-term fulfillment and the far-term fulfillment are seen by the prophet as being contiguous events; however, they are actually separated by centuries or even millennia. Whereas the end-time or eschatological fulfillment is complete, the near-term fulfillment is partial and serves as a foreshadowing of the final fulfillment. For example, read the following passage.

> **Isaiah 9:6-7**. For a child will be born for us, a son will be given to us, and the government will be on His shoulders. He will be named Wonderful Counselor, Mighty God, Eternal Father, Prince of Peace. The dominion will be vast, and its prosperity will never end. He will reign on the throne of David and over his kingdom, to establish and sustain it with justice and righteousness from now on and forever. The zeal of the Lord of Hosts will accomplish this.

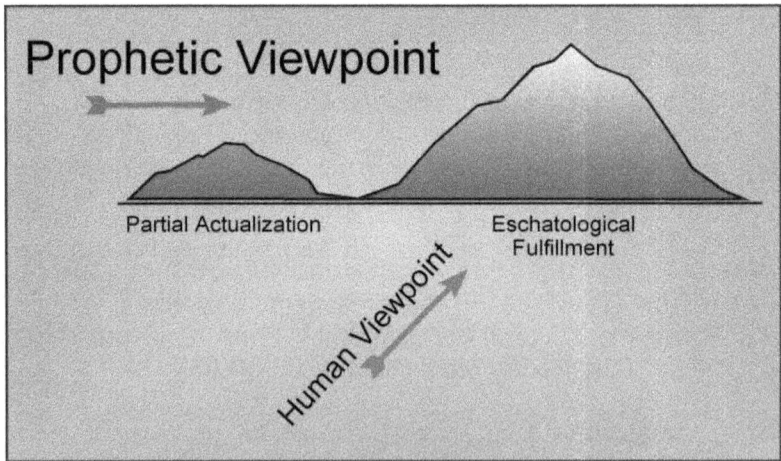

Figure 4. Double Vision: The Present Age and the Age to Come

Q 1. Which part of this prophecy has already been fulfilled and how?

Q 2. Which part has yet to be fulfilled?

Isaiah saw the first and second comings of Messiah as if they were a single event, like the mountain range in the distance appearing as part of the nearer range. However, in their actual fulfillment, the two events are distinct and separated by two millennia and still counting. Messiah's first coming is like the nearer mountain range, and His second coming is like the more distant mountain range.

Decoding the Symbols

Another key to understanding prophetic literature lies in decoding the rich symbolism. To do this, we must look at how the symbols are used elsewhere in the Bible. Consider the following example from the 4th chapter of Revelation:

> **Revelation 4:7.** ... The first living creature was like a lion; the second living creature was like a calf; the third living creature had a face like a man; and the fourth living creature was like a flying eagle.

Q 3. Describe the four living creatures identified in this passage together with the context of the passage.

Now let's consider another passage in the 1st chapter of Ezekiel which also describes living creatures with four faces:

> **Ezekiel 1:10.** The form of each of their faces was that of a man, and each of the four had the face of a lion on the right, the face of an ox on the left, and the face of an eagle.

Q 4. Describe the four living creatures identified in this passage together with the context of the passage.

Q 5. How are these two passages related, and what is their significance?

The four living creatures of Revelation 4 are found worshiping at God's throne, while the living creatures of Ezekiel 1 were part of the vision of God's glory. In both cases, the four faces of the beasts – the lion, the ox, the man, and the eagle – represent Jesus Christ as king (lion), suffering servant (ox), Son of Man (man), and Son of God (eagle) as set forth in the Gospels of Matthew, Mark, Luke, and John, respectively.

More Symbols in the Book of Revelation

Keep in mind that prophecy sheds light on prophecy. So when studying the symbols and word pictures in the Book of the Revelation, you will want to consider the prophecies of Ezekiel, Daniel and Zechariah.

Although prophecy may be challenging because of its symbolism and multiple fulfillments, we should be able to identify the overarching principle that is being communicated. In the Book of Revelation, it is the image of Christ presented in the 1st chapter that defines the theme and thrust of the entire book. This image portrays the Lord Christ as a colossus who stands in the midst of His church, represented by seven lamp stands. He holds the messengers or pastors of the seven churches in His right hand as He marches forward in righteous judgment against all who would threaten or harm His beloved bride, the church. The visions presented in the rest of the book develop and enlarge upon this initial vision as it relates to the trials and oppression faced by the church, both at the time of the writing of the book at the end of the 1st century and at the times of the end.

In this concluding section of our discussion of apocalyptic literature in the Bible, we will address ourselves to symbols encountered in the 12th and 13th chapters of Revelation. To prepare for this discussion, you should at least peruse the following:

> Chapter 12 of TR2 in which I discuss the events and circumstances associated with the second coming of Jesus Christ.

> The entire prophecy of Daniel.

> The 12th and 13th chapters of Revelation.

Q 6. What does the woman in the 12th chapter of Revelation represent? Explain your answer.

Q 7. Identify the male child of the woman and explain your answer.

Q 8. Who are the other children of the woman? Explain your answer.

Q 9. What does the red dragon represent? Consider the heads and horns mentioned in Revelation 12:3 and compare this vision with that revealed in Daniel 7:7. What significance do you derive from this comparison?

Q 10. What is the meaning of Revelation 12:4? Explain your answer.

Although seemingly difficult, the study of apocalyptic literature can be very rich and rewarding. Concerning the Book of the Revelation, godly men have spent a lifetime in its study, and many books have been written on how to best interpret it. Although there is a diversity of opinion on the details, some facts are clear. Jesus Christ is coming again, and when He comes He will...

Wed His bride, the church,

Judge sinners and bring about the final resolution to the problem of evil, sin and death,

Establish His kingdom on earth.

Amen; even so come, Lord Jesus!

Notes & Reflections

Session 8. Review and Discussion

This study on discovering the meaning of Scripture has been designed to train and equip you with the essential skills needed to rightly handle the word of truth in accordance with Paul's instruction to Timothy in 2 Timothy 2:15. While many would regard this study as the barest of introductions to the subject of biblical hermeneutics, we believe it is sufficient to project you, the student, onto a path of lifelong devotion to the careful study, interpretation, and application of God's word to your life and ministry. We have also endeavored to expand and enrich your appreciation for the Bible as a literary masterpiece through which God has once for all communicated His glorious redemptive purpose for mankind.

We discovered that correctly identifying genre and context are important prerequisites to discovering the author's intended meaning of a verse or passage, which is the necessary precursor for deriving from it appropriate applications to our lives and ministries.

> *While the meaning intended by the author is singular, the possible applications of that meaning to life and ministry are manifold.*

> *We must never read into Scripture what we think it says; rather, we must always allow it to speak for itself.*

Rightly handling the word of truth and properly applying it to life and ministry as directed by the Holy Spirit is, indeed, a great and challenging responsibility. Learning and practicing the skill to do this well is thoroughly worthwhile, as it enables us to share the truth of Scripture with accuracy, courage, and conviction.

As you strive to derive principles from Scripture for governing life and ministry, consider the following:

Is this principle normative? In other words, does it apply to all people, periods, and places? Or is it bound to a particular cultural and historical context?

71

Studying Scripture is like peeling an onion. The more layers you remove, the more truth you discover.

Spend time thinking and reflecting on passages being studied to allow the Holy Spirit to expand and enrich your insights, as well as give direction for application to your life and ministry.

Seize upon opportunities to engage in substantial theological discussion with other disciples; that is, do theology in community.

Use of Extra-Biblical Resources

While use of extra-biblical resources, such as a concordance, Bible dictionary, Bible handbook, and commentaries, are very useful, they should never be given the weight of Scripture itself. In general, the further removed a given resource is from the passage under study, both in a literary sense and in a chronological or historical sense, the less weight it should have. So, start with the immediate context of the passage under study, and then explore progressively larger circles of context.

Recommended Resources

Chapter 4 in the companion theological reader, TR1, will deepen, expand, and enrich your insights in regard to rightly handling the word of truth. Also, TR4 includes several appendices that are relevant to this area of study.

We recommend the use of either of the following two study Bibles:

The English Standard Version (ESV) Study Bible
The Holman Christian Standard (HCSB) Study Bible
Also, the Archaeological Study Bible helpfully provides useful archaeological, cultural, and historical context.

The following resources are available online:

Online versions of the ESV and HCSB Study Bibles
www.BibleHub.com
www.BlueLetterBible.org
www.BibleStudyTools.com

Discussion Questions

Q 1. For each of the four primary literary genres (narrative, poetry, didactic, and apocalyptic) select a paragraph-length passage to analyze. For each selected passage, discuss:

Your method of analysis, including context and literary genre.

Your interpretation of the passage.

Any theological, moral, or ethical principles you derived from the passage.

Q 2. For each of the four principle literary genres, discuss how the application of what you have learned from this study will shape and enrich your approach to studying the Bible.

Q 3. Discuss the impact of what you have learned upon your future life and ministry.

Notes & Reflections

Afterword

WitW is a product of Daystar Institute of Biblical Theology and

Leadership Development (DI), which is dedicated to supporting local churches in fulfillment of their mission of making disciples of all nations. We have two offices: DI / NM is based in Albuquerque, New Mexico, and DI / A is based in Kampala, Uganda. Please do not hesitate to contact us at www.DaystarInstitute/NM.us if you have any questions or comments or wish to request training in the use of our materials.

Peter Briggs is founder and president-emeritus of Daystar Institute of Biblical Theology & Leadership Development. In addition to teaching and mentoring, Dr. Briggs has authored the WitW Study Guide Series to challenge students in uncompromising discipleship, practical Christian theology, and building a biblical worldview. The WitW study has had a great impact in both East Africa and the USA and is an excellent tool for encouraging and equipping disciples of Jesus to actually live out their faith.

Dedication

The *Walking in the Way of Christ & the Apostles Study Guide Series* is dedicated to Reverend Morris Wanje, whose prayers for God to raise up a means for strengthening and equipping young pastors and church leaders in East Africa caused the Holy Spirit of God to move upon the hearts of godly men and women at Daystar Institute/NM to create this study.

Acknowledgments

I am grateful for the heroic efforts of our team of contributors, editors, board of directors, and all who have had a part in the development of the WitW study. In particular, I extend my heartfelt gratitude to my wife, Rosemarie, our daughter, Ruthanne Hamrick, and ministry associates John & Marcie Kinzer, Stephen Patterson, and Michael & Antoninah Mutinda, for their valuable input and help with the Study Guide Series; and to Darienne Dumas and Emily Fuller for proof-reading the texts.

Testimonials

"The *Walking in the Way of Christ & the Apostles* (WitW) series by Dr. Peter Briggs is a powerful tool for fulfilling Jesus' universal mandate to make disciples. WitW is theologically sound, conceptually brilliant, and life- changing for those who are trained by it. The impact of WitW is not only personal transformation into the image of Christ, but also a profound influence on families, churches, and the larger culture, whether in America or Africa or anywhere else. Peter Briggs is a theologian of substantial import, but he has not merely plied his theological craft in the halls of academia. With God's enablement, he has managed to translate biblical truth and disciple-making principles into something that actually works in the real world! Those who embrace and employ *Walking in the Way* in their own lives will find themselves part of a movement affecting generations to come."

Steven Collins, PhD, Executive Dean, Trinity Southwest University

"*Walking in the Way of Christ & the Apostles* (WitW) is a magnificent literary work in biblical theology that offers the student an education in practical Christianity. The WitW study was first introduced in November 2011; since that time we have been using it to instruct ministry leaders and rural pastors at a low cost, and the transformation of lives is phenomenal. Learners get to understand the message of the Bible and are able to study it effectively. In my own interaction with the material since 2012, I have come to realize that Jesus Christ is using it to revive His remnant in Kenya and other parts of Africa, teaching us how to think in a biblical way and be successful in all spheres of life. I am convinced that the WitW material holds the key to Africa's revival, and, in Yahweh's hand, it is a mighty tool for returning the continent back to Him."

Michael Mutinda, Team Leader, Daystar Institute / Africa

Walking in the Way of Christ & the Apostles
Study Guide Series

Part 1: Foundational Principles. These principles are foundational to equip the Christ-follower to have and to be governed by the mind of Christ.

1. The Way of God
2. The Storyline of the Bible
3. Biblical Reality
4. Discovering the Meaning of Scripture
5. Torah: The Fountainhead of Wisdom
6. The Two-Part Christian Gospel

Part 2: The Gospel of the Kingdom of God. Here we explore the ways in which the Christian gospel confronts the prideful rebellion of the human heart and exalts Christ as King over all.

7. Authority of the King
8. Called by the King
9. The Meaning of Discipleship
10. Disciplines of the Kingdom
11. Household of the King
12. The Second Coming of the King

Part 3 – The Gospel of God. This final set explores how the Christian gospel affords a complete solution to human depravity and the threefold problem of sin and death.

13. Introduction to the Gospel of God
14. The Reason for the Gospel of God
15. Content of the Gospel of God
16. Perversions of the Gospel of God
17. Application of the Gospel of God

Theological Readers (TR)

TR1 – Part 1: Foundational Principles
TR2 – Part 2: The Gospel of the Kingdom of God
TR3 – Part 3: The Gospel of God
TR4 – Resources and Appendices

Theological Handbooks (TH)

TH1 – Part 1: The Way of God
TH2 – Part 2
TH3 – Part 3

Connect with us at www.DaystarInstituteNM.us, or
Contact us via email at WalkingintheWayUSA@gmail.com